Little Big Giant

Stories of Wisdom and Inspiration

Madonna

Queen of Pop

Copyright © 2024 Little Big Giant

All rights reserved.

No part of this publication may be reproduced, stored in a retrieval system, or transmitted in any form or by any means, electronic, mechanical, photocopying, recording, or otherwise, without the prior written permission of the publisher.

Printed in the United States of America

First Edition: 2024

This copyright page includes the necessary copyright notice, permissions request information, acknowledgments for the cover design, interior design, and editing, as well as the details of the first edition.

www.littlebiggiant.com

Introduction

In the summer of 1984, a young singer named Madonna took the world by storm with her hit single "Like a Virgin." The provocative lyrics and seductive dance moves caused a stir among conservative groups, but it was her unapologetic attitude and fearless style that truly captivated audiences.

As she rose to fame, Madonna became a symbol of female empowerment and sexual liberation. Her music and image challenged societal norms and sparked conversations about gender roles and sexuality. But behind the glitz and glamour, there was a darker side to Madonna's rise to fame.

Rumors swirled about her tumultuous relationships and wild partying, but it wasn't until her infamous performance at the 1984 MTV Video Music Awards that the truth was revealed. During her performance of "Like a Virgin," Madonna suffered a wardrobe malfunction that left her exposed to millions of viewers.

The incident caused a media frenzy and cemented Madonna's status as a controversial and boundary-pushing artist. But it also raised questions about the price of fame and the sacrifices one must make to stay on top.

As the world watched in shock and fascination, one thing became clear: Madonna was not just a pop star, she was a force to be reckoned with. And her story was far from over.

Table of Contents

Table of Contents..7
Chapter 1..9
Early Years: Growing Up in Michigan......................9
Chapter 2..15
Discovering Her Passion for Music........................ 15
Chapter 3..21
Rising to Fame: The Release of "Like a Virgin"..... 21
Chapter 4..28
Controversy and Criticism: Madonna's Bold Image... 28
Chapter 5..35
Reinvention: From "Material Girl" to "Vogue"......... 35
Chapter 6..42
Marriage and Motherhood: Balancing Personal Life and Career.. 42
Chapter 7..50
Evolution of Music and Style: From Pop to Electronica... 50

Chapter 8..**57**
Humanitarian Efforts: Madonna's Impact on Social Issues...57

Chapter 9..**65**
Legacy and Influence: Madonna's Enduring Impact on Pop Culture.. 65

Chapter 10..**72**
Continuing Success: Madonna's Ongoing Music and Career Achievements...72

Chapter 1

Early Years: Growing Up in Michigan

Madonna was born on August 16, 1958, in Bay City, Michigan. She was the third of six children in her family. Her parents, Silvio Anthony Ciccone and Madonna Louise Fortin, were both of Italian descent. Madonna's father worked as an engineer and her mother was a homemaker.

Growing up in Michigan, Madonna was a curious and creative child. She loved to dance and sing, and would often put on performances for her family. She also enjoyed playing with her siblings and exploring the outdoors.

One of Madonna's favorite childhood memories was going to the Detroit Zoo with her family. She loved seeing all the different animals and learning about them. This sparked her interest in nature and animals, which would later inspire some of her music and performances.

Madonna attended St. Frederick's and St. Andrew's Catholic elementary schools, where she excelled in both academics and extracurricular activities. She was a straight-A student and participated in school plays and musicals. Her teachers and classmates remember her as a hardworking and talented student.

    As a child, Madonna also had a strong connection to her Catholic faith. She attended mass regularly with her family and even considered becoming a nun at one point. However, as she got older, she began to question some of the strict rules and teachings of the Catholic Church.

Key Takeaway: Madonna's early years in Michigan shaped her into the creative and curious person she is today. Her love for music, nature, and her Catholic faith were all important influences in her life.

Chapter 2

Discovering Her Passion for Music

Madonna was always a curious and energetic child. She loved to dance and sing, and her parents often found her putting on performances for her siblings and friends. But it wasn't until she was eight years old that she discovered her true passion for music.

One day, while rummaging through her parents' record collection, Madonna stumbled upon an album by the legendary singer, Aretha Franklin. She was immediately captivated by the powerful and soulful voice of the Queen of Soul. Madonna listened to the album over and over again, memorizing every lyric and trying to imitate Franklin's vocal style.

From that moment on, Madonna knew that she wanted to be a singer just like Aretha Franklin. She begged her parents to let her take singing lessons, and they finally gave in to her persistence. Madonna's vocal coach was impressed by her natural talent and dedication, and she quickly progressed in her lessons.

But Madonna didn't just want to be a singer, she wanted to be a performer. She would spend hours in front of the mirror, practicing her dance moves and perfecting her stage presence. Her hard work paid off when she landed a role in a local community theater production of "Annie."

Madonna's love for music continued to grow as she got older. She started writing her own songs and performing at school talent shows. Her classmates were amazed by her talent and encouraged her to pursue a career in music.

Key Takeaway: Madonna's passion for music was ignited when she discovered the powerful voice of Aretha Franklin. She worked hard to develop her own talents and never gave up on her dream of becoming a singer and performer. This teaches us that with hard work and dedication, we can achieve our goals and follow our passions.

Chapter 3

Rising to Fame: The Release of "Like a Virgin"

Madonna had been working tirelessly to make a name for herself in the music industry. She had already released her debut album, but it wasn't until her second album, "Like a Virgin," that she truly skyrocketed to fame.

The album was released on November 12, 1984, and it was an instant hit. Madonna's iconic image on the album cover, with her bleached blonde hair and bold red lips, caught the attention of everyone. But it wasn't just her looks that captivated the world, it was her music.

The title track, "Like a Virgin," was an upbeat and catchy tune that had people singing and dancing along. The lyrics were controversial at the time, but that only added to the buzz surrounding Madonna. She wasn't afraid to push boundaries and challenge societal norms, and that's what made her stand out from other artists.

The album also featured other hit songs such as "Material Girl" and "Dress You Up." Madonna's unique voice and style shone through in each song, and it was clear that she was a force to be reckoned with in the music industry.

"Like a Virgin" quickly climbed the charts, and Madonna's fame grew with each passing day. She was everywhere - on the radio, on TV, in magazines. Her music videos were a hit as well, with their bold and provocative visuals. Madonna was becoming a household name, and she was only just getting started.

But with fame came criticism. Madonna's risqué image and lyrics were met with backlash from some, but she didn't let that stop her. She continued to push boundaries and express herself through her music, and her fans loved her for it.

Key Takeaway: Madonna's release of "Like a Virgin" marked a turning point in her career. It solidified her as a music icon and set the stage for her future success. She showed that being true to yourself and not being afraid to take risks can lead to great things.

Chapter 4

Controversy and Criticism: Madonna's Bold Image

Madonna's rise to fame was not without its fair share of controversy and criticism. From the beginning, she made a name for herself as a bold and daring performer, pushing the boundaries of what was considered acceptable in the music industry. Her image, both on and off stage, often sparked heated debates and divided opinions among the public.

One of the most controversial moments in Madonna's career was her 1989 music video for the song "Like a Prayer."

The video featured religious imagery and themes, including burning crosses and stigmata, which caused outrage among religious groups. Many accused Madonna of blasphemy and called for a boycott of her music. Despite the backlash, the song became a huge hit and solidified Madonna's reputation as a provocative artist.

In the 1990s, Madonna continued to push the envelope with her music and performances. Her infamous "Blonde Ambition" tour featured provocative dance moves and revealing costumes, which drew criticism from conservative groups and parents. She also tackled taboo topics in her music, such as sexuality and feminism, which sparked debates and discussions among her fans and critics.

But perhaps the most controversial aspect of Madonna's image was her constant reinvention and evolution. She was never afraid to take risks and try new things, both in her music and her personal style. This often led to criticism from those who felt she was trying too hard or not staying true to her roots. However, Madonna's ability to constantly reinvent herself and stay relevant in the ever-changing music industry is a testament to her talent and determination.

    Despite the controversy and criticism, Madonna remained unapologetic and true to herself. She used her platform to challenge societal norms and push for change, especially when it came to issues of gender and sexuality. Her bold image and fearless attitude inspired a generation of young girls to be confident and unafraid to be themselves.

Key Takeaway: Madonna's bold image and unapologetic attitude showed the world that it's okay to be different and challenge societal norms. She taught us to embrace our individuality and use our voices to make a difference.

Chapter 5

Reinvention: From "Material Girl" to "Vogue"

Madonna had become a household name with her catchy tunes and daring fashion choices. She was known as the "Material Girl" and her music videos were constantly played on MTV. But as Madonna grew older, she realized that she needed to reinvent herself in order to stay relevant in the ever-changing music industry.

     With the release of her album "Like a Prayer" in 1989, Madonna showed the world that she was more than just a pop star. She tackled controversial topics such as religion and racism in her music, causing both praise and backlash from the public. This was just the beginning of Madonna's journey of reinvention.

In the early 1990s, Madonna's image took a drastic turn as she embraced a more provocative and sexual persona. She released her book "Sex" which featured explicit photos of herself, causing even more controversy. But this reinvention only solidified Madonna's status as a boundary-pushing artist.

In 1992, Madonna starred in the film "A League of Their Own" and received critical acclaim for her performance. This marked the beginning of her successful acting career, proving that she was a multi-talented artist.

But it was in 1998 that Madonna truly reinvented herself with the release of her album "Ray of Light". She traded in her signature pop sound for a more electronic and spiritual sound, showcasing her growth and maturity as an artist. The album was a huge success and won four Grammy Awards.

Madonna continued to reinvent herself with each album, exploring different genres and pushing the boundaries of music and art. She even ventured into the world of fashion, launching her own clothing line and collaborating with top designers.

But perhaps Madonna's most iconic reinvention came with the release of her hit song "Vogue" in 1990. The song, which paid homage to the underground dance culture of New York City, became a worldwide sensation and solidified Madonna as a trendsetter and style icon.

Key Takeaway: Madonna's reinvention taught us that it's important to embrace change and evolve as a person. She showed us that it's okay to take risks and push boundaries, even if it means facing criticism. Madonna's constant reinvention not only kept her relevant in the music industry, but also inspired others to be fearless and true to themselves.

Chapter 6

Marriage and Motherhood: Balancing Personal Life and Career

Madonna was at the height of her career, with hit songs and sold-out concerts all over the world. But as she reached her late 20s, she started to feel a different kind of longing – the desire to settle down and start a family.

After dating several famous men, Madonna finally found love in actor Sean Penn. They got married in 1985 in a lavish ceremony that was the talk of the town. But as their marriage progressed, it became clear that balancing their personal lives and careers would be a challenge.

As Madonna's music career continued to soar, Sean's acting career was facing some setbacks. This led to tension and arguments between the couple, and they eventually divorced in 1989. But their marriage was not without its happy moments, as they welcomed their first child, daughter Lourdes, in 1996.

After her divorce, Madonna focused on her music and continued to push boundaries with her provocative performances and bold fashion choices. But she also made time for her personal life, dating and eventually marrying director Guy Ritchie in 2000. They welcomed their son, Rocco, in the same year.

    With a growing family and a successful career, Madonna had to learn how to balance her personal life and career. She often brought her children on tour with her, making sure they were always close by. And when she wasn't on tour, she made sure to spend quality time with her children, being a hands-on mother and involving them in her creative projects.

But as her children grew older, Madonna faced new challenges. She had to navigate the delicate balance of being a mother to teenagers while also being a pop icon. She faced criticism for her parenting choices, but she always stayed true to herself and her beliefs.

Despite the challenges, Madonna has managed to successfully balance her personal life and career. She continues to be a devoted mother to her children, while also creating music and performing on stage. She has shown that with hard work, determination, and love, anything is possible.

Key Takeaway: Balancing personal life and career can be challenging, but with dedication and love, it is possible to have both a successful career and a fulfilling personal life. Madonna's story teaches us the importance of staying true to ourselves and our beliefs, even in the face of criticism.

Chapter 7

Evolution of Music and Style: From Pop to Electronica

Madonna's music and style have always been evolving, and in the late 1990s, she took a bold step into the world of electronica. This marked a significant change in her sound and image, as she embraced the futuristic beats and sounds of electronic music.

With her album "Ray of Light" released in 1998, Madonna introduced her fans to a whole new side of her music. The album featured songs like "Frozen" and "Ray of Light" that were heavily influenced by electronic beats and synthesizers. This was a departure from her previous pop sound, and it was met with both praise and criticism from fans and critics alike.

But Madonna didn't stop there. In 2000, she released her album "Music" which further solidified her foray into electronica. The album's title track became an instant hit, with its catchy beat and electronic sound. Madonna also incorporated elements of dance and techno into her live performances, showcasing her versatility as an artist.

Not only did Madonna's music evolve, but her style also underwent a transformation during this time. She embraced a more futuristic and edgy look, with metallic and neon colors, and bold geometric shapes. Her iconic "cowgirl" look from the "Music" era, with its cowboy hat and bedazzled bra, became an instant fashion statement.

But Madonna's evolution didn't stop there. In 2005, she released her album "Confessions on a Dance Floor" which was a nod to her disco roots. This album was a perfect blend of pop and electronica, with songs like "Hung Up" and "Sorry" dominating the charts. Madonna also collaborated with renowned DJ and producer Stuart Price, further cementing her place in the world of electronica.

Madonna's foray into electronica not only showcased her ability to adapt and evolve with the ever-changing music industry, but it also opened doors for other artists to experiment with electronic sounds. Her influence on the music scene cannot be denied, and she continues to inspire and push boundaries with her music and style.

Key Takeaway: Madonna's transition into electronica showed her versatility as an artist and paved the way for other musicians to explore and experiment with different genres. It's important to embrace change and try new things, just like Madonna did, in order to grow and evolve.

Chapter 8

Humanitarian Efforts: Madonna's Impact on Social Issues

Madonna is not only known for her iconic music and performances, but also for her passion and dedication towards making a positive impact in the world. Throughout her career, she has used her platform and influence to bring attention to important social issues and to support various humanitarian causes. Let's take a closer look at Madonna's impact on social issues and how she has made a difference in the world.

One of the causes that Madonna has been actively involved in is the fight against HIV/AIDS. In the 1980s, when the disease was still highly stigmatized and misunderstood, Madonna was one of the first celebrities to speak out about it. She used her music and performances to spread awareness and raise funds for research and treatment. In 1991, she even founded the non-profit organization Raising Malawi, which works to support children affected by HIV/AIDS in the African country of Malawi.

In addition to her work with HIV/AIDS, Madonna has also been a strong advocate for women's rights. She has spoken out against gender inequality and has used her voice to empower women all over the world. In 2013, she launched the "Art for Freedom" project, which aimed to raise awareness about women's rights and encourage people to take action. Through this project, Madonna collaborated with other artists and activists to create thought-provoking videos and artwork that shed light on important issues such as violence against women and gender discrimination.

Another cause that Madonna has been passionate about is education. She believes that every child deserves access to quality education, regardless of their background or circumstances. In 2006, she co-founded the Raising Malawi Academy for Girls, a school in Malawi that provides education and opportunities for girls who are at risk of being denied an education. Madonna has also supported various education initiatives in other parts of the world, including her home country of the United States.

Madonna's humanitarian efforts have not gone unnoticed. In 2013, she received the "Billboard Woman of the Year" award for her philanthropic work. She has also been recognized by organizations such as the United Nations and amfAR (The Foundation for AIDS Research) for her contributions to various causes.

Key Takeaway: Madonna's impact on social issues shows us that one person can make a difference in the world. By using her voice and platform, she has raised awareness and funds for important causes and has inspired others to take action. Her dedication and passion for making a positive impact serve as a reminder that we all have the power to create change and make the world a better place.

Chapter 9

Legacy and Influence: Madonna's Enduring Impact on Pop Culture

Madonna, the Queen of Pop, has been a dominant force in the music industry for over four decades. Her impact on pop culture is undeniable and her legacy continues to influence generations of artists. From her music to her fashion choices, Madonna has always pushed boundaries and challenged societal norms. Let's take a closer look at her enduring impact on pop culture.

Music:

Madonna's music has been a major influence on the pop genre. She has sold over 300 million records worldwide, making her one of the best-selling music artists of all time. Her songs, such as "Like a Virgin," "Vogue," and "Material Girl," have become iconic and are still played on the radio today. Madonna's ability to constantly reinvent herself and adapt to changing music trends has allowed her to stay relevant and influential in the industry.

Fashion:

Madonna's fashion choices have also left a lasting impact on pop culture. From her iconic cone bra to her signature fingerless gloves, Madonna's style has been imitated by countless fans and other artists. She has also been a pioneer in blending fashion with music, often using her music videos and performances as a platform to showcase her unique and daring fashion sense.

Social Issues:

Throughout her career, Madonna has used her platform to address important social issues. She has been a vocal advocate for the LGBTQ+ community, women's rights, and HIV/AIDS awareness. Her music and performances have often sparked conversations and debates, shedding light on important issues and bringing them to the forefront of popular culture.

Key Takeaway: Madonna's enduring impact on pop culture is a result of her fearlessness and determination to break barriers. She has shown that being different and standing out is something to be celebrated, and her influence continues to inspire generations of artists to be true to themselves and push boundaries.

Chapter 10

Continuing Success: Madonna's Ongoing Music and Career Achievements

Madonna's success in the music industry continued to soar as she released more albums and embarked on world tours. Her music evolved with each album, showcasing her versatility and creativity as an artist. She continued to push boundaries and challenge societal norms, solidifying her status as a cultural icon.

In 1990, Madonna released her album "The Immaculate Collection," which featured her greatest hits and became the best-selling compilation album by a solo artist in history. This album cemented her status as a music legend and proved that her music had a timeless appeal.

In the 1990s, Madonna also ventured into acting and received critical acclaim for her roles in films such as "Dick Tracy" and "Evita." She proved that she was not just a talented musician, but also a versatile actress.

In 1998, Madonna released her album "Ray of Light," which showcased a more spiritual and introspective side of her. The album was a commercial and critical success, earning her multiple Grammy Awards. She continued to experiment with her music and released more albums that were met with both commercial and critical success.

Madonna's career achievements also extended beyond music and acting. She founded her own record label, Maverick Records, in 1992 and signed talented artists such as Alanis Morissette and The Prodigy. She also ventured into fashion and launched her own clothing line, Material Girl, in 2010.

Despite facing controversies and criticism throughout her career, Madonna remained resilient and continued to push boundaries. She became the best-selling female artist of all time, with over 300 million records sold worldwide. She also holds the record for the highest-grossing solo touring artist of all time.

Key Takeaway: Madonna's ongoing success in the music industry is a testament to her talent, hard work, and determination. She has proven that with passion and perseverance, one can achieve greatness and leave a lasting impact on the world.

Dear Reader,

Thank you for choosing "Little Big Giant - Stories of Wisdom and Inspiration"! We hope this book has inspired and motivated you on your own journey to success.

If you enjoyed reading this book and believe in the power of its message, we kindly ask for your support. Please consider leaving a positive review on the platform where you purchased the book. Your review will help spread the message to more young readers, empowering them to dream big and achieve greatness. We acknowledge that mistakes can happen, and we appreciate your forgiveness.

Remember, the overall message of this book is the key. Thank you for being a part of our mission to inspire and uplift young minds.

Printed in Great Britain
by Amazon